easy
Japanese

THE AUSTRALIAN
Women's Weekly

CONTENTS

japanese ingredients   4

japanese essentials   6

starters   8

poultry   26

seafood   34

beef & pork   44

noodles   54

vegetables   64

glossary   74

conversion chart   77

index   78

AUSTRALIAN CUP AND
SPOON MEASUREMENTS
ARE METRIC. A
CONVERSION CHART
APPEARS ON PAGE 77.

You can hardly walk a block in any city centre without passing a sushi shop or noodle bar. This book will help you to make your favourite sushi at home, and encourage you to experiment with more unusual Japanese dishes. Not only is Japanese food delicious but it is also low in fat, deceptively simple to prepare and beautiful in its presentation.

Pamela Clark

Food Director

JAPANESE BREADCRUMBS (PANKO)

Available in two kinds (large and fine), they are bigger than traditional breadcrumbs and make a very crisp coating for deep-fried food.

JAPANESE PEPPER

Ground seeds of the Japanese prickly ash, it has a spicy aroma and flavour, and a slightly numbing quality, like sichuan pepper, which you can use if you cannot find japanese pepper.

BONITO FLAKES

Dried, smoked and cured bonito (a type of tuna) is shaved into flakes and sold as large or fine flakes. Large flakes are used to make dashi, while fine flakes are used as a garnish. It has a strong aroma but a smoky, mellow flavour. Store in an airtight container.

NORI SEAWEED

Nori is a dried laver seaweed which grows on rocks in bays and at the mouths of rivers. Crisp paper-like sheets of compressed seaweed are commonly used to wrap sushi. It is sometimes sold pre-toasted (yaki-nori); if not, place in large frying pan or under grill to toast quickly on one side until crisp. It also comes finely shredded or as flakes (ao-nori) for sprinkling as a garnish.

JAPANESE INGREDIENTS

SEVEN-SPICE MIX

It always includes togarashi, a red-hot japanese chilli. The remaining six ingredients are flexible but often include mustard seeds, sesame seeds, poppy seeds, sansho pepper, shiso and nori flakes.

WAKAME SEAWEED

Wakame is a highly nutritious seaweed that is black when it is purchased dried, but reconstitutes to a bright green colour. Soak for only 5 minutes or it will go mushy. The leaves are usually stripped from the central vein.

DRIED KELP SEAWEED (KONBU)

This is the basis of dashi. Sold in wide strips, it often has a white powdery substance that coats the surface. Wipe with a damp cloth to discard any grit but do not wipe clean or rinse, so as not to remove surface flavour. It develops a bitter flavour if overcooked, so always remove just before water boils. To enhance flavour, cut along edges before adding to water.

MISO

Fermented soybean paste, miso is available in different grades, colours and strengths. Generally, the darker the miso, the saltier the taste and denser the texture. Two main types are used: white (shiro) which has a sweet mild flavour and gold colour; and red (aka) which is more earthy and salty, and is a dark caramel colour. Store in an airtight container for up to one year in the refrigerator.

SESAME SALT (GOMASIO)

prep + cook time 20 minutes (+ cooling) makes ¼ cup
nutritional count per tablespoon 6.5g total fat
(0.8g saturated fat); 297kJ (71 cal); 0.1g carbohydrate;
2.6g protein; 1.2g fibre

Dry-fry ¼ cup white sesame seeds in medium
frying pan until toasted; cool. Blend, process or
grind seeds and 1 teaspoon salt until coarse.
gomasio is an excellent seasoning for rice,
soups, stews and vegetables.

tip **If using an electric blender, do not overprocess, as
you want a grainy texture, not a paste.**

RED MISO SAUCE

prep + cook time 10 minutes (+ cooling) makes ½ cup
nutritional count per tablespoon 1g total fat
(0.1g saturated fat); 305kJ (73 cal); 13.1g carbohydrate;
2.2g protein; 0.9g fibre

Stir ⅓ cup water, ¼ cup white miso, ¼ cup
mirin, ¼ cup caster (superfine) sugar,
1½ tablespoons light soy sauce and
1 tablespoon red miso in small saucepan over
low heat until sugar dissolves; cool 5 minutes.

tip **Add some crushed dried chilli for extra flavour.
This sauce is typically served as an accompaniment
to tofu and vegetables.**

JAPANESE ESSENTIALS

PICKLED GINGER

prep + cook time **25 minutes (+ standing)** makes **2 cups**
nutritional count per tablespoon **0.1g total fat**
(0g saturated fat); 184kJ (44 cal);
10.2g carbohydrate; 0.2g protein; 0.6g fibre

Peel and thinly slice 500g (1 pound) fresh
ginger. Combine ginger and 1 tablespoon salt
in medium bowl; stand 1 hour. Rinse ginger
under cold running water; drain. Stir 1½ cups
white vinegar and 1 cup caster (superfine)
sugar in medium saucepan over heat, without
boiling, until sugar dissolves. Bring to the boil.
Add ginger; return to the boil. Bottle in sterilised
jars; seal.

tip **To sterilise jars, place clean open jars and lids in**
preheated oven at 120°C/250°F for 15 minutes. Remove
from oven when ready to fill.

TEMPURA DIPPING SAUCE

prep + cook time **10 minutes** makes **2¾ cups**
nutritional count per tablespoon **0g total fat**
(0g saturated fat); 13kJ (3 cal); 0.2g carbohydrate;
0.2g protein; 0g fibre

Bring 1¼ cups water, ½ teaspoon dashi
granules, ⅓ cup japanese soy sauce and
¼ cup mirin to the boil in small saucepan.
Reduce heat to low; keep warm until ready
to serve.

BEEF SALAD

prep + cook time 20 minutes serves 4
nutritional count per serving 15.9g total fat
(3.9g saturated fat); 1116kJ (267 cal);
2g carbohydrate; 27.4g protein; 0.5g fibre

1 tablespoon vegetable oil
2 beef fillet steaks (500g)
100g (3 ounces) baby rocket leaves
1 green onion (scallion), sliced thinly
mustard and soy dressing
2 tablespoons japanese soy sauce
1 tablespoon rice vinegar
1 tablespoon sake
1 tablespoon olive oil
1 teaspoon caster (superfine) sugar
½ teaspoon japanese mustard
½ teaspoon sesame oil
2cm (¾-inch) piece fresh ginger (10g), grated
1 clove garlic, crushed

1 Heat oil in heavy-based frying pan; cook
steak until well browned. Plunge steak into
bowl of iced water; remove steak, pat dry with
absorbent paper.
2 Make mustard and soy dressing.
3 Slice beef thinly; arrange on plates. Top with
rocket; drizzle over dressing. Sprinkle with
green onion.
mustard and soy dressing Combine
ingredients in small bowl.

tip To make this recipe a light main course for two,
serve it with steamed rice or noodles.

STARTERS

HAND-MOULDED SUSHI

prep + cook time **20 minutes** makes **30**
nutritional count per piece **0.3g total fat**
(0.1g saturated fat); 171kJ (41 cal);
5.9g carbohydrate; 3.6g protein; 0.1g fibre

3 cups prepared sushi rice
   (see recipe, page 13)
350g (11-ounce) piece sashimi tuna,
   sliced thinly
2 teaspoons wasabi paste
¼ cup (60ml) japanese soy sauce

1 Dip fingers in bowl of vinegared water
(see tips); shake off excess. Pick up about
1 tablespoon of rice with one hand, gently
squeezing and shaping it into a rectangular
shape with rounded edges.
2 Pick up one slice of fish with index finger and
thumb of left hand. Using tip of right-hand
index finger, scoop up a dab of wasabi; spread
wasabi along centre of fish.
3 Bend fingers of left hand to form cup to hold
fish; place rice shape on fish. Move left thumb
to top end of rice shape to stop rice being
pushed off fish; use right-hand index and
middle fingers to gently push rice shape and
fish together.

4 Turn sushi piece over in left hand, so fish
is on top. Gently push fish against rice with
right-hand index and middle fingers; left thumb
should remain at top end of rice to stop it
being pushed out.
5 With thumb on one side of rice and index
finger on the other, gently squeeze rice to
straighten the sides.
6 Using right-hand index finger and thumb,
turn sushi 180 degrees and push fish
against rice again with right-hand index and
middle fingers.
7 Serve sushi with sauce.
tips **For rice vinegared water, add 1 tablespoon rice**
vinegar to medium bowl of cold water.
To keep fish on rice, place a 1cm (½-inch) wide strip of
toasted seaweed (yaki-nori) around centre of sushi
piece with ends tucked underneath; moisture from the
rice will hold seaweed in place.
If correctly formed, hand-moulded sushi should be able
to be eaten upside down using fingers, or on its side,
if eaten with chopsticks. It's the fish and not the rice
which is to be dipped in soy sauce.

sushi rice

SUSHI RICE

prep + cook time 25 minutes (+ standing) makes 9 cups
nutritional count per 1 cup 0.3g total fat
(0.1g saturated fat); 1091kJ (261 cal);
58.8g carbohydrate; 4.4g protein; 0.5g fibre

3 cups (600g) japanese rice (koshihikari)
3 cups (750ml) water
sushi vinegar
½ cup (125ml) rice vinegar
¼ cup (55g) caster (superfine) sugar
½ teaspoon salt

1 Place rice in large bowl, cover with cold water, stir with hand; drain. Repeat process two or three times until water is almost clear. Drain rice in strainer at least 30 minutes.
2 Meanwhile, make sushi vinegar.
3 Place rice and the water in medium saucepan, cover tightly; bring to the boil. Reduce heat; simmer, covered tightly, on low heat about 12 minutes or until water is absorbed. Remove from heat; allow rice to stand, covered, 10 minutes.
4 Spread rice in large, non-metallic, flat-based bowl or tub (preferably wood). Using large flat wooden spoon or plastic spatula, repeatedly slice through rice at sharp angle to break up lumps and separate grains, gradually pouring in sushi vinegar. Not all of the vinegar may be required; rice shouldn't become too wet or mushy. Continue to slice through rice (don't stir because it crushes the grains) with one hand, lifting and turning rice from outside into centre.
5 Meanwhile, using other hand, fan rice until it is almost cool; this will take about 5 minutes (an electric fan, on the low setting, can be used instead of a hand-held fan, if you prefer). Do not over-cool rice or it will harden. Performing these two actions together will give you glossy, slightly sticky, but still separate, sushi rice. Keep rice covered with damp cloth to stop it drying out while making sushi.
sushi vinegar Stir ingredients in small bowl until sugar dissolves.
tips Sushi vinegar can be made ahead; refrigerate in an airtight container. You could also use ½ cup (125ml) ready-made bottled sushi vinegar.
For a slightly less astringent mixture, heat it gently just before using.

tuna sashimi

TUNA SASHIMI

prep time 10 minutes (+ standing) serves 4
nutritional count per serving 2.2g total fat
(0.5g saturated fat); 635kJ (152 cal);
4g carbohydrate; 27.8g protein; 0.9g fibre

200g (6½ ounces) daikon, shredded finely
400g (12½-ounce) piece sashimi tuna
2 teaspoons wasabi paste
2 tablespoons (35g) drained pink
    pickled ginger
⅓ cup (80ml) japanese soy sauce

1 Place daikon in medium bowl, cover with iced water, stand 15 minutes; drain.
2 Place tuna on chopping board; using very sharp knife, cut 6mm (¼-inch) slices at right angle to the grain of the fish, holding piece of skinned fish with your fingers and slicing with knife almost vertical to the board.
3 Divide tuna and daikon among serving plates; serve with wasabi, ginger and sauce.
tip Use a mandoline, if you have one, to shred daikon.

chicken yakitori

CHICKEN YAKITORI

prep + cook time 30 minutes (+ refrigeration) makes 24
nutritional count per skewer 0.6g total fat
(0.1g saturated fat); 121kJ (29 cal);
0.3g carbohydrate; 4.9g protein; 0g fibre

500g (1 pound) chicken breast fillets,
   sliced thinly
½ cup (125ml) mirin
¼ cup (60ml) kecap manis
1 tablespoon japanese soy sauce
1 teaspoon white sesame seeds, toasted
1 green onion (scallion), sliced thinly

1 Thread chicken loosely onto skewers; place,
in single layer, in large shallow dish.
2 Combine mirin, kecap manis and sauce in
small jug. Pour half the marinade over skewers;
reserve remaining marinade. Cover skewers;
refrigerate 3 hours or overnight.
3 Simmer reserved marinade in small
saucepan over low heat until reduced by half.

4 Meanwhile, cook drained skewers on
heated oiled grill plate (or grill or barbecue) until
cooked through.
5 Serve skewers drizzled with hot marinade;
sprinkle with seeds and onion.
tip You need 24 bamboo skewers for this recipe.
Soak them in cold water for an hour before use to
prevent them from scorching during cooking.

GYOZAS (POT STICKERS)

prep + cook time 30 minutes (+ refrigeration) makes 50
nutritional count per gyoza 1.2g total fat
(0.3g saturated fat); 142kJ (34 cal);
3.4g carbohydrate; 2.1g protein; 0.4g fibre

325g (10½ ounces) cabbage, chopped finely
300g (9½ ounces) minced (ground) pork
4 green onions (scallions), chopped finely
1 egg, beaten lightly
2 tablespoons japanese soy sauce
1 tablespoon sake
2 teaspoons sesame oil
1 teaspoon caster (superfine) sugar
¼ teaspoon white pepper
50 gyoza wrappers
1 tablespoon vegetable oil

1 Combine cabbage, pork, onion, egg, sauce,
sake, sesame oil, sugar and pepper in medium
bowl. Cover; refrigerate 1 hour.
2 Place one heaped teaspoon of pork mixture
in centre of one wrapper. Wet edge around
one half of wrapper; pleat to seal. Repeat with
remaining pork mixture and wrappers.
3 Cover base of large frying pan with water;
bring to the boil, then add gyozas, in batches.
Reduce heat; simmer, covered, 3 minutes.
4 Heat vegetable oil in same cleaned pan;
cook gyozas, one side only, uncovered, in
batches, until browned and slightly crisp.
Drain on absorbent paper.
tips You can vary the filling of these dumplings by
adding chopped prawns (shrimp), cheese, capsicum
(bell pepper) or scrambled egg.
Serve with soy sauce mixed with chilli oil, or
rice vinegar.

gyozas (pot stickers)

salmon and shiitake soup

SALMON AND SHIITAKE SOUP

prep + cook time **40 minutes** serves **4**
nutritional count per serving **1.7g total fat**
(0.5g saturated fat); 288kJ (69 cal);
6.4g carbohydrate; 6.1g protein; 1.6g fibre

1kg (2 pounds) salmon bones and heads
1 small brown onion (80g), quartered
1.25 litres (5 cups) water
¼ cup (60g) white miso
4 fresh shiitake mushrooms, sliced thinly
2 teaspoons fresh ginger juice
16 snow pea sprouts, trimmed
80g (2½ ounces) daikon, shredded finely

1 Place salmon bones and heads in large
saucepan with onion and the water. Bring to
the boil. Reduce heat; simmer, uncovered,
20 minutes. Remove any scum from surface of
stock; strain stock mixture through muslin-lined
strainer into large bowl. Return stock to same
cleaned pan.
2 Place miso in small bowl, gradually add
1 cup (250ml) of the hot stock, stirring,
until miso dissolves. Add to saucepan;
stir to combine.
3 Add mushrooms, return to a simmer.
Remove from heat; stir in juice. Serve soup
topped with sprouts and daikon.
tips Simmer stock after straining for a stronger flavour.
You can use red miso instead of white. Red miso is
stronger and saltier, so only use about 2 tablespoons
in this recipe.
To obtain ginger juice, squeeze grated fresh ginger into
a sieve set over a bowl. A piece of ginger measuring
about 10cm (4 inches) in length will yield 2 tablespoons
of grated ginger which, in turn, should yield the
2 teaspoons of juice used in this recipe.

egg drop soup

EGG DROP SOUP

prep + cook time **10 minutes** serves **4**
nutritional count per serving **3.5g total fat**
(1.2g saturated fat); 297kJ (71 cal);
2g carbohydrate; 7g protein; 0g fibre

1 litre (4 cups) water
1½ teaspoons dashi granules
1 tablespoon mirin
1 tablespoon light soy sauce
2 teaspoons japanese soy sauce
2 eggs, beaten lightly
2 green onions (scallions), sliced thinly

1 Bring the water and dashi to the boil in large
saucepan. Stir in mirin and sauces; gradually
stir in egg.
2 Serve soup sprinkled with onion.
tip You can add 100g (3 ounces) cooked green beans
for a more substantial soup.

somen and dashi broth

THICK OMELETTE

prep + cook time 15 minutes (+ cooling) serves 4
nutritional count per serving 21.2g total fat
(4.8g saturated fat); 1133kJ (271 cal);
3.6g carbohydrate; 16.5g protein; 0.2g fibre

8 eggs, beaten lightly
1 tablespoon water or dashi
2 teaspoons caster (superfine) sugar
3 teaspoons mirin
2 teaspoons light soy sauce
2 tablespoons vegetable oil
⅓ cup (80ml) japanese soy sauce
60g (2 ounces) daikon, grated finely

1 Stir egg, the water or dashi, sugar, mirin and light soy in large jug until sugar dissolves.
2 Heat a little of the oil in a traditional square frying pan or medium (20cm/8-inch) frying pan over medium heat. Pour in enough egg mixture to just cover base of pan; cook, tilting pan to spread mixture evenly. Break any large air bubbles, so omelette lies flat. When mixture is almost set, run spatula around edge of pan to loosen omelette.
3 Starting from back of pan, fold omelette into three towards front of pan. Gently push folded omelette to back of pan.
4 Lightly oil pan again, repeat process, lifting up the cooked omelette, so egg mixture runs underneath it. When nearly cooked, fold in three, starting with the omelette already cooked and folded. Repeat this step until all mixture is used.
5 Tip omelette onto bamboo mat and wrap firmly to form a compact rectangle. Cool omelette; cut into 1cm (½-inch) slices. Serve with japanese soy and daikon.
tip Sliced omelette can also be used for sushi or cut lengthways into long, thin strips and used as a filling for sushi rolls. To give a colourful centre, wrap the first omelette around cooked carrot and green onion (scallion).

SOMEN AND DASHI BROTH

prep + cook time 20 minutes serves 6
nutritional count per serving 0.2g total fat
(0g saturated fat); 297kJ (71 cal);
12.1g carbohydrate; 2.3g protein; 0.7g fibre

3 dried shiitake mushrooms
100g (3 ounces) dried somen noodles
1.5 litres (6 cups) water
2 tablespoons sake
2 tablespoons mirin
2 tablespoons light soy sauce
2 teaspoons dashi granules
2 tablespoons finely shredded lemon rind

1 Place mushrooms in small heatproof bowl, cover with boiling water, stand 20 minutes; drain. Discard stems; slice caps thinly.
2 Meanwhile, cook noodles in medium saucepan of boiling water until tender; drain.
3 Bring the water, sake, mirin, sauce and granules to the boil in large saucepan. Reduce heat; simmer, uncovered, 10 minutes.
4 Divide noodles, mushrooms and rind among bowls; ladle over broth.

thick omelette

sashimi rolls

SASHIMI ROLLS

prep + cook time 20 minutes   makes 18
nutritional count per roll 0.2g total fat (0g saturated fat);
67kJ (16 cal); 0.2g carbohydrate; 3.2g protein; 0.1g fibre

200g (6½-ounce) piece sashimi fish
½ lebanese cucumber (65g)
1 green onion (scallion), green part only
¼ medium red capsicum (bell pepper) (50g),
    sliced thinly
¼ cup (60ml) japanese soy sauce

1 Sharpen knife using a steel; wipe knife.
Cut fish into paper-thin slices.
2 Halve cucumber lengthways; scrape out
seeds with teaspoon and discard. Cut cucumber
and onion into long, thin strips; trim strips to
same size as width of fish slices.
3 Place fish slice on board. Place one or two
pieces of each vegetable at one end; roll fish to
enclose filling. Repeat with remaining fish and
filling. Serve rolls with sauce.

tips We used a combination of red (salmon), oily (tuna)
and white (snapper) fish for this recipe, but you could
also use trevally or various other types, as long as all are
labelled "sashimi-quality" at your fishmonger or market.
Ask your fishmonger to slice it thinly for you, if you
prefer not to do so yourself.
When serving mixed sashimi, it is important that the
different types of fish do not touch each other.
A toasted nori sheet, a few garlic chives or blanched
spinach leaves can also be used, trimmed to the same
size as each piece of fish.

SPICY TERIYAKI TUNA

prep + cook time 45 minutes (+ refrigeration) makes 24
nutritional count per spoon 0.9g total fat
(0.3g saturated fat); 138kJ (33 cal);
2.2g carbohydrate; 3.6g protein; 0.1g fibre

¾ cup (180ml) japanese soy sauce
¼ cup (60ml) mirin
2 tablespoons honey
1 tablespoon wasabi paste
1 teaspoon sesame oil
300g (9½-ounce) piece sashimi tuna
2 tablespoons (46g) drained pink pickled
    ginger, sliced thinly

spicy teriyaki tuna

1 Combine sauce, mirin, honey, wasabi and oil
in medium bowl; reserve ½ cup of marinade in
small jug. Add tuna to the medium bowl; turn
tuna to coat in marinade. Cover; refrigerate
3 hours or overnight.
2 Drain tuna; discard marinade. Cook tuna in
heated oiled medium frying pan until browned
both sides and cooked as you like (do not
overcook, as tuna has a tendency to dry out).
Cut tuna into 24 cubes.
3 Place chinese spoons on serving platter.
Place one piece of tuna in each spoon;
top with 1 teaspoon of the reserved marinade
and a little ginger.

tip Chinese spoons are available from Asian food stores.

california rolls

1 Lightly beat egg and sake in small bowl until combined. Heat oil in wok. Pour egg mixture into wok; cook, tilting wok, until egg is almost set. Remove omelette from wok; roll tightly, slice thinly. Cool to room temperature.

2 Place one sheet of seaweed, shiny-side down, on sushi mat. Using damp fingers, spread half the rice over seaweed, leaving 4cm (1¾-inch) border at one end.

3 Layer omelette, crab, daikon, carrot and cucumber over centre of rice.

4 Using mat, roll firmly to form sushi roll. Place roll, seam-side down, on board; using sharp knife, cut roll into six mini-maki pieces.

5 Repeat with remaining seaweed, rice, omelette, crab, daikon, carrot and cucumber. Serve with sauce, ginger and wasabi.

CALIFORNIA ROLLS

prep + cook time 30 minutes (+ cooling) makes 12
nutritional count per roll 1.1g total fat
(0.3g saturated fat); 364kJ (87 cal);
16.1g carbohydrate; 2.5g protein; 0.4g fibre

1 egg
1 teaspoon sake
1 teaspoon oil
2 sheets toasted seaweed (yaki-nori)
3 cups prepared sushi rice
   (see recipe, page 13)
2 crab sticks (40g), cut into strips
25g (¾ ounce) pickled daikon, cut into strips
4cm (1¾-inch) piece carrot (25g),
   cut into strips
4cm (1¾-inch) piece cucumber (25g),
   cut into strips
¼ cup (60ml) japanese soy sauce
2 tablespoons (46g) drained pink
   pickled ginger
2 teaspoons wasabi paste

SCALLOPS WITH MISO SAUCE

prep + cook time 20 minutes serves 4
nutritional count per serving 15.4g total fat
(4.5g saturated fat); 890kJ (213 cal);
8.8g carbohydrate; 7.1g protein; 2.9g fibre

12 scallops (300g), roe removed
1 clove garlic, crushed
2 tablespoons plain (all-purpose) flour
1 tablespoon vegetable oil
2 tablespoons dry white wine
1 tablespoon white miso
1 tablespoon mirin
1 teaspoon japanese soy sauce
1 teaspoon caster (superfine) sugar
1 tablespoon water
2 tablespoons double cream
2 teaspoons wholegrain mustard
200g (6½ ounces) watercress,
   chopped coarsely

1 Combine scallops and garlic in small bowl. Toss in flour; shake away excess.

2 Heat oil in medium frying pan; cook scallops both sides until browned lightly. Remove from pan; cover to keep warm.

3 Add wine, miso, mirin, sauce, sugar and the water to same pan; bring to the boil. Remove pan from heat; stir in cream and mustard until combined.

4 Serve scallops with sauce and watercress.

scallops with miso sauce

TUNA ROLLS

prep + cook time **20 minutes** makes **36**
nutritional count per roll **0.2g total fat**
(0.1g saturated fat); 130kJ (31 cal);
5.2g carbohydrate; 1.9g protein; 0.1g fibre

3 sheets toasted seaweed (yaki-nori)
3 cups prepared sushi rice
  (see recipe, page 13)
1 tablespoon wasabi paste
200g (6½-ounce) piece sashimi tuna,
  cut into thick strips
2 tablespoons (46g) drained pink
  pickled ginger
¼ cup (60ml) japanese soy sauce

1 Fold one sheet of seaweed in half
lengthways, parallel with lines on rough side;
cut along fold. Place a half sheet, shiny-side
down, lengthways across bamboo mat, about
2cm (¾-inch) from side closest to you.
2 Dip fingers in bowl of rice vinegared water
(see tip); shake off excess. Pick up about
½ cup of the rice; squeeze into oblong shape,
place across centre of seaweed. Wet fingers
again, then gently "rake" rice evenly from left
to right, leaving 2cm (¾-inch) border on far end
of seaweed. Build up rice in front of border to
form a mound, to keep filling in place.

3 Swipe a dab of wasabi across centre of
rice, flattening it out evenly. Place tuna strips,
end to end, in a row over wasabi, across
centre of rice.
4 Starting with side closest to you, pick up
mat using thumb and index fingers of both
hands; use remaining fingers to hold filling in
place as you begin to roll mat away from
you. Roll forward, pressing gently but tightly,
wrapping seaweed around rice and filling.
With roll seam-side down, gently press it
slightly into a square shape
5 Unroll mat; place sushi roll, seam-side down,
on board. Wipe very sharp knife with damp
cloth, then cut roll in half. Turn one piece
around, so that the two cut ends of each
half are aligned. Cut rolls together into thirds,
wiping knife between each cut, to give a total
of six pieces.
6 Working quickly, repeat process with
remaining seaweed halves, rice and tuna,
using a dab of wasabi with each.
7 Serve tuna rolls with remaining wasabi,
pickled ginger and sauce.
tip **For rice vinegared water, add 1 tablespoon rice**
vinegar to medium bowl of water.

SAKE DUCK WITH SNOW PEAS AND AVOCADO

prep + cook time 25 minutes serves 2
nutritional count per serving 43.2g total fat
(10.8g saturated fat); 2291kJ (548 cal);
11.1g carbohydrate; 23.8g protein; 2.2g fibre

100g (3 ounces) snow peas
½ medium red capsicum (bell pepper) (100g),
    sliced thinly
1 tablespoon olive oil
200g (6½ ounces) single duck breast fillet
¼ cup (60ml) sake
2 tablespoons light soy sauce
1 tablespoon light brown sugar
1 tablespoon rice vinegar
½ small avocado (100g), chopped

1 Boil, steam or microwave peas and
capsicum until just tender; drain. Rinse under
cold water; pat dry with absorbent paper.
2 Heat oil in medium frying pan; cook duck,
skin-side down, until skin is browned and crisp.
Turn duck; cook 5 minutes or until duck is
tender. Remove duck from pan; stand
10 minutes. Slice thinly.
3 Meanwhile, combine sake, sauce, sugar
and vinegar in clean pan; simmer, uncovered,
2 minutes or until sauce is thick and syrupy.
4 Remove syrup from heat; add duck, turn to
coat. Serve duck with snow peas, capsicum
and avocado.

POULTRY

grilled miso chicken

GRILLED MISO CHICKEN

prep + cook time **15 minutes** (+ refrigeration) serves **8**
nutritional count per serving **11.2g** total fat
(3.4g saturated fat); 953kJ (228 cal);
1.7g carbohydrate; 28.9g protein; 0.4g fibre

8 chicken thigh fillets (1.2kg)
2 tablespoons light soy sauce
2 tablespoons sake
2 tablespoons mirin
2 tablespoons white miso
2 green onions (scallions), chopped finely
1cm (½-inch) piece fresh ginger (5g), grated
1 clove garlic, crushed

1 Place chicken and combined remaining ingredients in shallow dish, rubbing marinade all over chicken. Cover; refrigerate 1 hour.
2 Drain chicken; reserve marinade. Cook chicken on heated oiled grill plate (or grill or barbecue), brushing with reserved marinade, about 6 minutes on each side or until cooked through.
3 Serve chicken with steamed rice and a sprinkle of seven-spice mix, if you like.

CRISP DUCK BREAST WITH ORANGE AND DAIKON SALAD

prep + cook time **30 minutes** (+ refrigeration) serves **4**
nutritional count per serving **60.4g** total fat
(16.6g saturated fat); 3214kJ (769 cal);
12.4g carbohydrate; 41.6g protein; 3.9g fibre

3 medium oranges (720g)
300g (9½ ounces) daikon
1½ tablespoons vegetable oil
1 teaspoon sesame oil
1 tablespoon sake
4 duck breasts (800g), skin scored
1 teaspoon salt
80g (2½ ounces) rocket (arugula) or mizuna
ponzu dressing
5cm (2-inch) piece kelp (konbu), shredded
1 tablespoon japanese soy sauce
1 tablespoon sake
1 teaspoon rice vinegar
1 teaspoon mirin
1 teaspoon bonito flakes

crisp duck breast with orange and daikon salad

1 Make ponzu dressing.
2 Segment oranges over salad bowl; reserve 1 tablespoon of juice. Using vegetable peeler, slice daikon into ribbons.
3 Strain ponzu dressing into small bowl; add oils, sake and reserved juice.
4 Season duck with salt, rubbing well into skin. Cook duck, skin-side down, in heated oiled frying pan until skin is golden. Remove from pan; discard fat. Return duck to same pan; cook until done to your liking. Remove duck from pan; stand, covered, 5 minutes. Slice thinly.
5 Meanwhile, place drained orange in medium bowl with daikon and rocket; toss gently to combine.
6 Serve duck with salad; drizzle with dressing.
ponzu dressing Combine ingredients in small non-metallic bowl. Refrigerate overnight.

sake-marinated quail

3 Drain quails; reserve marinade. Heat oil in large saucepan; deep-fry quails, in batches, until browned and tender. Remove from pan. Drain on absorbent paper; keep warm.
4 Meanwhile, bring reserved marinade to the boil in frying pan. Reduce heat; simmer until reduced by one third. Stir in blended cornflour and stock; stir until sauce boils and thickens.
5 Serve quail with sauce.

CHICKEN AND NOODLE SALAD

prep + cook time 30 minutes serves 4
nutritional count per serving 29.3g total fat
(5.2g saturated fat); 2976kJ (712 cal);
55.9g carbohydrate; 43g protein; 8.1g fibre

500g (1 pound) chicken thigh fillets
200g (6½ ounces) snake beans,
    cut into chunks
300g (9½ ounces) dried udon noodles
80g (2½ ounces) baby tat soi leaves
2 cups loosely packed fresh coriander
    (cilantro) leaves
sesame and peanut dressing
½ cup (75g) white sesame seeds, toasted
½ cup (75g) roasted unsalted peanuts
½ cup (125ml) mirin
⅓ cup (80ml) sake

1 Place chicken in medium saucepan of boiling water; return to the boil. Reduce heat; simmer, uncovered, about 10 minutes or until cooked through. Cool chicken in poaching liquid 10 minutes; discard liquid. Slice chicken thinly.
2 Meanwhile, boil, steam or microwave beans until just tender; drain. Rinse under cold water; drain.
3 Meanwhile, make sesame and peanut dressing.
4 Cook noodles in large saucepan of boiling water until tender; drain. Rinse under cold water; drain.
5 Place chicken, beans and noodles in large bowl with tat soi, coriander and dressing; toss gently to combine.
sesame and peanut dressing Blend or process ingredients until smooth.

SAKE-MARINATED QUAIL

prep + cook time 25 minutes (+ refrigeration) serves 6
nutritional count per serving 27.7g total fat
(6g saturated fat); 2157kJ (516 cal);
23.4g carbohydrate; 32.3g protein; 0.4g fibre

12 quails (2kg)
¾ cup (180ml) sake
⅔ cup (160ml) sweet sherry
½ cup (110g) light brown sugar
⅓ cup (80ml) light soy sauce
2 tablespoons mirin
3 green onions (scallions), chopped
8cm (3-inch) piece fresh ginger (40g), grated
4 cloves garlic, crushed
vegetable oil, for deep-frying
1 tablespoon cornflour (cornstarch)
½ cup (125ml) chicken stock

1 Tie quail legs with string; tuck wings under body. Bring large saucepan of water to the boil. Add quails to water in batches, simmer 2 minutes; drain quails, discard water.
2 Combine quails, sake, sherry, sugar, sauce, mirin, onion, ginger and garlic in large bowl. Cover; refrigerate 4 hours or overnight, turning quails occasionally.

chicken and noodle salad

STEAMED CHICKEN SALAD WITH SESAME SAUCE

prep + cook time 25 minutes serves 4
nutritional count per serving 13.4g total fat
(2.5g saturated fat); 890kJ (213 cal);
6.3g carbohydrate; 15.1g protein; 2.7g fibre

2 spring onions (50g)
2 lebanese cucumbers (260g)
250g (8 ounces) chicken thigh fillets,
    with skin
1 tablespoon sake
1 teaspoon sesame oil
1cm (½-inch) piece fresh ginger (5g), grated
sesame sauce
2 tablespoons sesame paste
1 tablespoon japanese soy sauce
1 tablespoon caster (superfine) sugar
1 tablespoon white sesame seeds,
    ground coarsely
1 teaspoon rice vinegar
1 teaspoon chilli paste
1cm (½-inch) piece fresh ginger (5g), grated
1 clove garlic, crushed

1 Chop onion finely, keeping white and green parts separate. Halve cucumber lengthways; cut into chunks.

2 Pierce chicken with skewer; place in medium microwave-safe bowl. Drizzle with sake and oil; sprinkle with white part of the onion and ginger. Cook, covered, in microwave (600 Watt) 4 minutes or until cooked through. Cool 5 minutes; reserve cooking liquid for sauce.

3 Make sesame sauce.

4 Shred chicken with hands. Place chicken in medium bowl with cucumber and sauce; toss gently to combine. Serve sprinkled with green part of the onion.

sesame sauce Whisk ingredients in small bowl, with 1½ tablespoons of the reserved cooking liquid, until smooth.

tip Sesame paste, which is available ready made, is traditionally made by grinding toasted sesame seeds to a rough paste in a mortar and pestle. Tahini (Greek-style sesame paste) is a reasonable substitute; however, it is not made from toasted sesame seeds, so there will be a difference in flavour.

SEAFOOD AND UDON NOODLE STIR-FRY

prep + cook time 25 minutes serves 4
nutritional count per serving 11.7g total fat
(1.5g saturated fat); 2332kJ (558 cal);
70.1g carbohydrate; 38.9g protein; 5.7g fibre

10 uncooked medium king prawns
   (shrimp) (450g)
400g (12½ ounces) dried udon noodles
2 tablespoons sunflower oil
4 small cleaned squid hoods (300g),
   cut into rings
100g (3 ounces) fresh shiitake mushrooms,
   sliced thinly
4 green onions (scallions), chopped coarsely
1 tablespoon shredded dried
   seaweed (ao-nori)
2½ cups (200g) bean sprouts, trimmed
⅓ cup bonito flakes
⅓ cup (80ml) japanese soy sauce

1 Shell and devein prawns.
2 Cook noodles in large saucepan of boiling
water until tender; drain. Rinse; drain.
3 Heat oil in wok; stir-fry squid and prawns
2 minutes. Add mushrooms, onion, seaweed
and half the sprouts; stir-fry 2 minutes. Add
noodles and remaining ingredients to wok;
stir-fry until hot. Serve topped with
remaining sprouts.

SEAFOOD

SEAFOOD TEMPURA

prep + cook time **40 minutes** serves **4**
nutritional count per serving **29.9g total fat**
(4.2g saturated fat); 3081kJ (737 cal);
67.9g carbohydrate; 45.9g protein; 4.5g fibre

12 uncooked medium king prawns
**   (shrimp) (540g)**
2 small cleaned squid hoods (150g)
2 medium brown onions (300g)
8 fresh shiitake mushrooms or large
**   button mushrooms**
2 sheets toasted seaweed (yaki-nori)
20g (¾ ounce) dried somen noodles,
**   cut in half**
vegetable oil, for deep-frying
12 scallops (300g), roe removed
300g (12½ ounces) thin white fish fillets,
**   cut into cubes**
1 small red capsicum (bell pepper) (150g),
**   cut into squares**
plain (all-purpose) flour, for dusting
1 quantity tempura batter (see recipe,
**   page 66)**
1 medium lemon (140g), cut into wedges

1 Shell and devein prawns, leaving tails intact. Make three small cuts on underside of each prawn, halfway through flesh, to prevent curling when cooked. Trim a thin edge off each tail and, with the back of a knife, gently press to expel any moisture that might make the oil spit during cooking.
2 Cut squid down centre to open out; score inside in diagonal pattern, then cut into large squares or strips.
3 Halve onions through root end. Insert toothpicks at regular intervals to hold onion rings together; slice in between. Discard mushroom stems; cut a cross in top of caps.
4 Cut one sheet seaweed into 5cm (2-inch) squares; halve the other sheet and cut into 2cm (¾-inch) wide strips. Brush seaweed strips with water and wrap tightly around middle of about 10 noodles; reserve noodle bunches.
5 Heat oil in large saucepan. Dust seafood and vegetables, except seaweed squares, lightly in flour; shake off excess flour. Dip seaweed squares and other ingredients in batter; drain excess. Deep-fry ingredients, in batches, until golden; drain on absorbent paper. Only fry small amounts at a time; make sure enough time is allowed for oil to come back to correct temperature before adding next batch.
6 Deep-fry reserved noodle bundles and serve as garnish. Serve with lemon wedges and warm tempura dipping sauce (see recipe, page 7).

salmon teriyaki

SALMON TERIYAKI

prep + cook time **20 minutes (+ standing)** serves **4**
nutritional count per serving **12.5g total fat**
(2.8g saturated fat); 1333kJ (319 cal);
7.2g carbohydrate; 36.7g protein; 0.5g fibre

120g (4 ounces) daikon, shredded finely
4 salmon fillets (700g), skinned
teriyaki marinade
⅔ cup (160ml) japanese soy sauce
⅔ cup (160ml) mirin
2 tablespoons sake
1 tablespoon caster (superfine) sugar

1 Place daikon in small bowl, cover with
iced water, stand 15 minutes; drain.
2 Meanwhile, make teriyaki marinade.
3 Combine salmon and marinade in medium
bowl; stand 10 minutes, turning occasionally.
4 Drain salmon over medium bowl; reserve
marinade. Cook salmon on heated oiled
grill plate (or grill or barbecue), brushing
occasionally with marinade, until cooked
as you like.
5 Bring reserved marinade to the boil in small
saucepan. Reduce heat; simmer 5 minutes
or until sauce thickens slightly.
6 Serve salmon with daikon; drizzle with sauce.
teriyaki marinade Stir ingredients in medium
bowl until sugar dissolves.

tip **Ready-made teriyaki sauce may be used, but it's
stronger than homemade. Dilute it with a little mirin,
sake or water, according to taste.**

sake-glazed salmon

SAKE-GLAZED SALMON

prep + cook time **20 minutes** serves **4**
nutritional count per serving **26.4g total fat**
(8.9g saturated fat); 1659kJ (397 cal);
2.6g carbohydrate; 34.7g protein; 0g fibre

1 tablespoon vegetable oil
1 teaspoon sesame oil
4 salmon fillets (700g), skin on
40g (1½ ounces) butter
¼ cup (60ml) sake
1½ tablespoons japanese soy sauce
1 tablespoon mirin
2 teaspoons caster (superfine) sugar
5mm (¼-inch) piece fresh ginger (2g), grated

1 Heat oils in large frying pan; cook salmon,
skin-side down, 3 minutes or until skin is
golden. Turn salmon; cook 2-3 minutes or until
rare. Remove from pan; cover to keep warm.
2 Discard oil from pan. Add butter, sake,
sauce, mirin, sugar and ginger; stir until sugar
dissolves. Bring to the boil; cook, stirring, about
2 minutes or until sauce thickens slightly.
3 Serve salmon drizzled with glaze.
tips **Check for bones; pull them out with clean tweezers.
Serve salmon with steamed rice and a green salad.**

salt and pepper salmon with wasabi mayonnaise

SALT AND PEPPER SALMON WITH WASABI MAYONNAISE

prep + cook time 25 minutes serves 4
nutritional count per serving 40.1g total fat
(6.3g saturated fat); 2278kJ (545 cal);
7.5g carbohydrate; 39.4g protein; 0.2g fibre

2 teaspoons sea salt
2 teaspoons japanese pepper
1½ tablespoons vegetable oil
4 salmon fillets (800g), skin on
½ cup (150g) mayonnaise
2 teaspoons wasabi paste
1 teaspoon finely chopped fresh
  coriander (cilantro)
1 teaspoon lime juice

1 Blend, process or grind salt and pepper until
fine. Combine pepper mixture, oil and salmon
in large bowl; stand 5 minutes.
2 Meanwhile, combine mayonnaise, wasabi,
coriander and juice in small bowl.
3 Cook salmon on heated oiled grill plate
(or grill or barbecue) until cooked to your liking.
4 Serve salmon with wasabi mayonnaise,
and watercress, if you like.

SEAFOOD HOT POT

prep + cook time 40 minutes serves 4
nutritional count per serving 7.8g total fat
(1.3g saturated fat); 2307kJ (552 cal);
57.3g carbohydrate; 56.8g protein; 4.5g fibre

12 medium black mussels (300g)
12 uncooked medium king prawns
  (shrimp) (540g)
12 scallops (300g), roe removed
400g (12½ ounces) firm white fish fillets,
  cut into cubes
⅓ cup (80ml) japanese soy sauce
⅓ cup (80ml) sake
2 teaspoons mirin
1 tablespoon vegetable oil
2 cloves garlic, crushed
5cm (2-inch) piece fresh ginger (25g),
  chopped finely
3 cups (750ml) fish stock
1 cup (250ml) water
1 teaspoon powdered dashi
1 small kumara (orange sweet potato) (250g),
  halved lengthways, sliced thinly
250g (8 ounces) spinach, chopped coarsely
2 green onions (scallions), chopped coarsely
270g (8½ ounces) dried udon noodles

1 Scrub mussels; remove beards. Shell and
devein prawns, leaving tails intact.
2 Combine mussels, prawns, scallops, fish,
1 tablespoon each of sauce and sake, and
mirin in large bowl.
3 Heat oil in large saucepan; cook garlic
and ginger, stirring, until fragrant. Add stock,
the water, dashi and remaining sauce and
sake; bring to the boil. Add kumara; cook,
uncovered, 2 minutes. Add undrained seafood;
cook, covered, about 5 minutes or until
mussels open (discard any that do not).
Add spinach and onion; cook, uncovered,
until spinach wilts.
4 Meanwhile, cook noodles in large saucepan
of boiling water until tender; drain.
5 Divide noodles among serving bowls;
top with seafood mixture.

seafood hot pot

marinated deep-fried snapper

MARINATED DEEP-FRIED SNAPPER

prep + cook time 30 minutes (+ standing) serves 4
nutritional count per serving 11.5g total fat
(1.9g saturated fat); 1204kJ (288 cal);
15.2g carbohydrate; 26.2g protein; 2.1g fibre

2 snapper fillets (500g)
2 tablespoons sake
2 tablespoons japanese soy sauce
1 tablespoon mirin
2cm (¾-inch) piece fresh ginger (10g), grated
¾ cup (75g) potato starch
vegetable oil, for deep-frying
1 green onion (scallion), sliced thinly
2 medium lemons (280g), cut into wedges

1 Check fish for bones; pull them out with clean
tweezers. Cut fish into 4cm (1½-inch) cubes.
2 Combine fish, sake, sauce, mirin and ginger
in medium bowl; stand 20 minutes.
3 Drain fish; discard marinade. Toss fish in
potato starch; shake off excess.
4 Heat oil in saucepan; deep-fry fish until crisp
and golden. Sprinkle with onion; serve with
lemon wedges.

tip Serve snapper with a tempura dipping sauce for
extra flavour (see recipe, page 7).

STEAMED SNAPPER
WITH WAKAME

prep + cook time 20 minutes (+ standing) serves 4
nutritional count per serving 7.2g total fat
(3.8g saturated fat); 924kJ (221 cal);
0.6g carbohydrate; 36g protein; 0.5g fibre

2 tablespoons dried seaweed (wakame)
4 snapper fillets (700g)
2 tablespoons sake
2 green onions (scallions), sliced thinly
20g (¾ ounce) butter
ginger and lemon dipping sauce
2cm (¾-inch) piece fresh ginger (10g), grated
1 tablespoon lemon juice
2 teaspoons japanese soy sauce
¼ teaspoon sesame oil

steamed snapper with wakame

1 Place seaweed in small bowl, cover with
cold water, stand 5 minutes; drain.
2 Place each fillet on a square of oiled baking
paper (parchment) or foil large enough to
completely enclose fish; top each fillet with
sake, seaweed, onion and butter. Gather
corners of paper squares together above fish;
twist to enclose securely.
3 Place parcels in large bamboo steamer.
Steam, covered, over wok or large frying
pan of simmering water about 10 minutes
or until fish is cooked through.
4 Meanwhile, make ginger and lemon
dipping sauce.
5 Serve fish with dipping sauce.
ginger and lemon dipping sauce Combine
ingredients in small bowl.

SESAME-ROASTED STEAK

prep + cook time 45 minutes (+ refrigeration) serves 4
nutritional count per serving 17.3g total fat
(5.2g saturated fat); 1459kJ (349 cal);
2g carbohydrate; 44.6g protein; 0.7g fibre

2 tablespoons white sesame seeds, toasted
2 tablespoons japanese soy sauce
1 tablespoon sake
1 teaspoon caster (superfine) sugar
2.5cm (1-inch) piece fresh ginger (15g), grated
1 clove garlic, crushed
4 beef scotch fillet steaks (800g)
3 green onions (scallions), cut into short
　　thin strips
1 tablespoon olive oil
chilli dressing
¼ cup (60ml) japanese soy sauce
1 teaspoon dashi granules
¼ teaspoon seven-spice mix
2cm (¾-inch) piece fresh ginger (10g),
　　sliced finely

1 Blend, process or grind seeds until coarse.
Combine seeds, sauce, sake, sugar, ginger
and garlic in shallow dish with steaks. Cover;
refrigerate 30 minutes.
2 Meanwhile, make chilli dressing.
3 Place onion in small bowl, cover with iced
water, stand 10 minutes or until crisp and
curled; drain.
4 Heat oil in large frying pan; cook steaks until
done to your liking. Remove from pan; stand
5 minutes, covered, to keep warm. Slice thickly.
5 Arrange sliced steaks on serving plate;
drizzle over dressing. Top with onion; serve
on steamed rice, if you like.
chilli dressing Combine ingredients in
small bowl.

BEEF &
PORK

TEPPANYAKI (MIXED BARBECUE)

prep + cook time **40 minutes (+ standing)** serves **4**
nutritional count per serving **11.8g total fat**
(4.2g saturated fat); 1580kJ (378 cal);
8.8g carbohydrate; 56.5g protein; 1.7g fibre

4 uncooked large king prawns
    (shrimp) (280g)
500g (1 pound) beef eye fillet, sliced thinly
350g (11 ounces) chicken breast fillet,
    skin on, cut into chunks
¼ cup (60ml) japanese soy sauce
2 cloves garlic, crushed
1 fresh small red thai (serrano) chilli,
    seeded, chopped finely
4 fresh shiitake mushrooms
1 medium onion (150g), sliced thinly
1 medium red capsicum (bell pepper) (200g),
    seeded and chopped
4 green onions (scallions), chopped finely
dipping sauce
½ cup (125ml) japanese soy sauce
1 tablespoon mirin
1 tablespoon light brown sugar
2cm (¾-inch) piece fresh ginger (20g), grated
½ teaspoon sesame oil

1 Shell and devein prawns, leaving tails intact.
Combine prawns with beef, chicken, sauce,
garlic and chilli in large bowl; stand 15 minutes.
2 Meanwhile, make dipping sauce.
3 Discard mushroom stems; cut a cross in
the top of caps.
4 Cook ingredients, except green onions,
in batches, on heated oiled grill plate (or grill
or barbecue) until vegetables are just tender,
prawns and beef are cooked as you like, and
chicken is cooked through.
5 Serve with green onion and individual bowls
of dipping sauce.
dipping sauce Stir ingredients in medium
saucepan until sugar dissolves.

tips You could use rump or sirloin steak instead of
the beef eye fillet.
Teppanyaki is traditionally cooked on a grill plate on
or near the table, and is eaten in batches; a portable
electric grill is ideal for this.

beef teriyaki platter

STIR-FRIED PORK AND GINGER CABBAGE

prep + cook time 25 minutes serves 4
nutritional count per serving 11.6g total fat
(2g saturated fat); 915kJ (219 cal);
2.8g carbohydrate; 23.5g protein; 1.7g fibre

400g (12½ ounces) pork fillet, cut into strips
¼ cup (60ml) japanese soy sauce
2 tablespoons sake
1 teaspoon caster (superfine) sugar
1cm (½-inch) piece fresh ginger (5g), grated
8 large wombok (napa cabbage) leaves
2 tablespoons vegetable oil
3 teaspoons fresh ginger juice

1 Combine pork, sauce, sake, sugar and grated ginger in medium bowl. Drain pork over small bowl; reserve marinade.
2 Discard thick ribs from wombok; cut leaves into 4cm (1½-inch) squares.
3 Heat oil in wok; stir-fry pork, in batches, until browned. Remove from wok.
4 Return pork to wok with cabbage, reserved marinade and juice; stir-fry until hot. Serve with steamed rice and top with chopped green onions, if you like.

tip To obtain ginger juice, squeeze grated fresh ginger into a sieve set over a bowl. A piece of ginger measuring about 15cm (6 inches) in length will yield 3 tablespoons of grated ginger; this amount of grated ginger should in turn yield the 3 teaspoons of juice used in this recipe.

BEEF TERIYAKI PLATTER

prep + cook time 30 minutes (+ refrigeration) serves 4
nutritional count per serving 11.6g total fat
(4.4g saturated fat); 1099kJ (263 cal);
4.7g carbohydrate; 34g protein; 1.7g fibre

600g (1¼ pounds) sirloin steaks, trimmed
⅓ cup (80ml) teriyaki sauce
2.5cm (1-inch) piece fresh ginger (15g), grated
1 clove garlic, crushed
500g (1 pound) thick asparagus, trimmed
8 thick green onions (scallions), trimmed
1 teaspoon wasabi paste
¼ cup (60ml) japanese soy sauce

1 Combine steaks, teriyaki sauce, ginger and garlic in large bowl. Cover; refrigerate 3 hours or overnight.
2 Drain steaks; discard marinade. Cook steaks on heated oiled grill plate (or grill or barbecue) until cooked as desired. Transfer steaks to warm plate; cover, stand 5 minutes.
3 Meanwhile, cook asparagus and onions on heated oiled grill plate (or grill or barbecue) until tender.
4 Slice steaks thinly. Place on warmed serving platter with asparagus, green onions, wasabi and sauce; serve with steamed rice, if you like.

stir-fried pork and ginger cabbage

teriyaki pork with pineapple

TERIYAKI PORK WITH PINEAPPLE

prep + cook time **40 minutes (+ refrigeration)** serves **4**
nutritional count per serving **4.6g total fat**
(1.4g saturated fat); 1078kJ (258 cal);
12.7g carbohydrate; 35.1g protein; 2.7g fibre

600g (1¼ pounds) pork fillets
⅓ cup (80ml) mirin
¼ cup (60ml) japanese soy sauce
2 tablespoons sake
2 teaspoons caster (superfine) sugar
5cm (2-inch) piece fresh ginger (25g), grated
2 cloves garlic, crushed
1 small pineapple (900g), sliced thinly
2 green onions (scallions), sliced thinly

1 Combine pork, mirin, sauce, sake, sugar, ginger and garlic in large bowl. Cover; refrigerate 3 hours or overnight.
2 Drain pork over small bowl; reserve marinade. Cook pork on heated oiled grill plate (or grill or barbecue) until browned and cooked to your liking. Remove from grill plate; cover to keep warm.
3 Cook pineapple slices on same grill plate until soft.
4 Bring reserved marinade to the boil in small saucepan; boil 5 minutes or until sauce reduces by half.
5 Serve sliced pork on pineapple, top with onion; drizzle with sauce.

japanese pork stir-fry

JAPANESE PORK STIR-FRY

prep + cook times **25 minutes** serves **4**
nutritional count per serving **15.9g total fat**
(3.2g saturated fat); 1409kJ (337 cal);
9.8g carbohydrate; 36.8g protein; 3.6g fibre

2 tablespoons peanut oil
600g (1¼ pounds) pork fillets, sliced thinly
1 large brown onion (200g), sliced thinly
200g (6½ ounces) green beans,
    chopped coarsely
1 medium red capsicum (bell pepper) (200g),
    sliced thinly
1 medium green capsicum (bell pepper)
    (200g), sliced thinly
2 cups (140g) coarsely shredded wombok
    (napa cabbage)
¼ cup (60ml) tonkatsu sauce
¼ cup (60ml) sukiyaki sauce

1 Heat half the oil in wok; stir-fry pork, in batches, until browned all over. Remove from wok.
2 Heat remaining oil in wok; stir-fry onion until soft. Add beans and capsicums; stir-fry until just tender.
3 Return pork to wok with wombok and sauces; stir-fry until wombok wilts.

DEEP-FRIED CRUMBED PORK (TONKATSU)

prep + cook time **30 minutes** serves **4**
nutritional count per serving **28.8g total fat**
(5.5g saturated fat); 2412kJ (577 cal);
32.4g carbohydrate; 43g protein; 5.1g fibre

300g (9½ ounces) cabbage, shredded finely
4 pork steaks (600g)
¼ cup (35g) plain (all-purpose) flour
2 eggs, beaten lightly
2 teaspoons water
2 cups (100g) japanese breadcrumbs
vegetable oil, for deep-frying
1 medium lemon (140g), cut into wedges
3 teaspoons japanese mustard
tonkatsu sauce
⅓ cup (80ml) tomato sauce (ketchup)
2 tablespoons japanese worcestershire sauce
2 tablespoons sake
1 teaspoon japanese soy sauce
1 teaspoon japanese mustard

1 Place cabbage in large bowl, cover with iced water, stand 5 minutes until crisp; drain.
2 Meanwhile, make tonkatsu sauce.
3 Pound pork gently with meat mallet. Coat pork in flour; shake off excess. Dip pork in combined egg and the water; coat in breadcrumbs.
4 Heat enough oil to cover pork in medium saucepan or deep-fryer. Cook pork, in batches, turning occasionally, about 5 minutes or until golden all over (skim oil between batches to remove any crumbs); drain on absorbent paper. Cut pork diagonally into 2cm (¾-inch) slices.
5 Place cabbage on serving plate; arrange pork slices on cabbage. Serve with lemon wedges, mustard and tonkatsu sauce.

tonkatsu sauce Bring ingredients to the boil in small saucepan; whisk until smooth. Remove from heat; cool.

tips Japanese breadcrumbs are available in two crumb sizes; either size is suitable for this recipe. Ready-made tonkatsu sauce is also available from Asian food stores.

FRIED SOBA

prep + cook time 35 minutes serves 4
nutritional count per serving 20g total fat
(3.9g saturated fat); 2274kJ (544 cal);
57g carbohydrate; 26.1g protein; 7.9g fibre

250g (8 ounces) dried soba noodles
1 tablespoon sesame oil
2 tablespoons vegetable oil
300g (9½ ounces) minced (ground) pork
1 medium brown onion (150g), cut into
    eight wedges
1 clove garlic, crushed
1cm (½-inch) piece fresh ginger (5g), grated
500g (1 pound) cabbage, shredded finely
1 medium red capsicum (bell pepper) (200g),
    sliced thinly
2 tablespoons (46g) drained red pickled ginger
2 teaspoons shredded seaweed (ao-nori)
sauce
¼ cup (60ml) mirin
¼ cup (60ml) japanese soy sauce
2 tablespoons sake
1 tablespoon caster (superfine) sugar

1 Cook noodles in large saucepan of boiling
water until tender; drain.
2 Make sauce.
3 Heat sesame oil and half the vegetable oil in
wok; stir-fry pork until browned lightly. Remove
from wok; cover to keep warm.
4 Heat remaining vegetable oil in wok; stir-fry
onion, garlic and fresh ginger until onion
softens. Add cabbage and capsicum; stir-fry
until tender. Add pickled ginger, pork, noodles
and sauce; stir-fry until hot. Serve sprinkled
with seaweed.
sauce Stir ingredients in small saucepan over
heat until sugar dissolves.

NOODLES

UDON NOODLE SOUP

prep + cook time **15 minutes** serves **4**
nutritional count per serving **3.3g total fat**
(0.9g saturated fat); 1822kJ (436 cal);
71.9g carbohydrate; 24.4g protein; 5.3g fibre

1.5 litres (6 cups) water
3 teaspoons dashi granules
2 small leeks (400g), sliced thinly
3 spring onions
200g (6½ ounces) pork loin, sliced thinly
⅓ cup (80ml) japanese soy sauce
2 tablespoons mirin
400g (12½ ounces) dried udon noodles

1 Bring the water and dashi granules to the
boil in large saucepan; add leek, return to the
boil. Reduce heat; simmer, uncovered, about
5 minutes or until tender.
2 Meanwhile, cut 2 spring onions into chunks;
thinly slice remaining onion. Add onion chunks,
pork, sauce and mirin to pan; simmer until pork
is cooked through.
3 Cook noodles in large saucepan of boiling
water until tender; drain.
4 Divide noodles and soup among bowls;
sprinkle with sliced onion. Serve sprinkled with
a little seven-spice mix, if you like.

tip **Be careful to not overcook the pork. It will cook very**
quickly if sliced thinly.

fried noodles

SOBA NOODLES WITH PORK, EGGPLANT AND CHILLI

prep + cook time **45 minutes** serves **4**
nutritional count per serving **26.6g total fat**
(6g saturated fat); 2504kJ (599 cal);
47.9g carbohydrate; 38.3g protein; 4.3g fibre

6 green onions (scallions)
¼ cup (60ml) vegetable oil
1 teaspoon sesame oil
3 baby eggplants (180g), sliced thickly
3 cloves garlic, crushed
2cm (¾-inch) piece fresh ginger (10g),
    grated finely
600g (1¼ pounds) minced (ground) pork
2 tablespoons mirin
2 tablespoons chilli bean paste
1 tablespoon tomato paste
1 tablespoons japanese soy sauce
1 teaspoon light brown sugar
½ teaspoon dashi granules
1 cup (250ml) water
250g (8 ounces) dried soba noodles

1 Slice onion diagonally, keeping white and green part separate.
2 Combine oils in bowl. Heat 2 tablespoons of the combined oils in wok; stir-fry eggplant until golden. Drain on absorbent paper.
3 Heat remaining combined oils in wok; stir-fry garlic, ginger and white part of the onion until fragrant. Remove from wok.
4 Stir-fry pork in wok until browned. Return garlic mixture to wok with mirin, pastes, sauce, sugar, dashi granules and the water; bring to the boil. Reduce heat; simmer 5 minutes.
5 Return eggplant with half the green part of onion. Simmer 3 minutes until eggplant is tender. Increase heat; boil about 5 minutes or until meat sauce thickens.
6 Meanwhile, cook noodles in large saucepan of boiling water until tender; drain. Rinse under cold water; drain.
7 Serve noodles topped with meat sauce; sprinkle with remaining onion.

FRIED NOODLES

prep + cook time **35 minutes** serves **4**
nutritional count per serving **15.9g total fat**
(3.1g saturated fat); 2153kJ (515 cal);
52.7g carbohydrate; 37.3g protein; 5g fibre

250g (8 ounces) dried wheat noodles
2 tablespoons peanut oil
500g (1 pound) pork fillets, sliced thinly
1 large brown onion (200g), sliced thinly
1 medium red capsicum (bell pepper) (200g),
    sliced thinly
1 medium green capsicum (bell pepper)
    (200g), sliced thinly
140g (5½ ounces) wombok (napa cabbage),
    shredded coarsely
¼ cup (60ml) tonkatsu sauce
¼ cup (60ml) sukiyaki sauce

1 Cook noodles in large saucepan of boiling water until tender; drain. Rinse under cold water; drain.
2 Meanwhile, heat half the oil in wok; stir-fry pork, in batches, until browned all over. Remove from wok.
3 Heat remaining oil in wok; stir-fry onion until soft. Add capsicums; stir-fry until tender.
4 Return pork to wok with noodles, wombok and sauces; stir-fry until hot.

soba noodles with pork, eggplant and chilli

RAMEN NOODLES WITH SOY BROTH

prep + cook time **6 hours**
(+ standing & refrigeration) serves **4**
nutritional count per serving **6.5g total fat**
(2.5g saturated fat); 1317kJ (315 cal);
38.4g carbohydrate; 19.1g protein; 6.1g fibre

8 dried shiitake mushrooms
500g (1 pound) fresh ramen noodles
⅓ cup (80ml) japanese soy sauce
⅓ cup (80ml) sake
100g (3 ounces) bamboo shoots, sliced thinly
125g (4 ounces) chinese barbecued pork,
    sliced thinly
500g (1 pound) baby buk choy, leaves
    separated, blanched
1 cup (80g) bean sprouts, trimmed
4 green onions (scallions), cut into chunks
soy broth
1kg (2 pounds) pork bones
1kg (2 pounds) chicken bones
10 spring onion bulbs, bruised
100g (3 ounces) fresh ginger, sliced
1 head garlic, halved widthways
2 medium carrots (240g), cut into chunks
10cm (4-inch) piece kelp (konbu)

1 Make soy broth.
2 Place mushrooms in small heatproof bowl,
cover with boiling water, stand 20 minutes;
drain. Discard stems.
3 Cook noodles in large saucepan of boiling
water, until tender; drain. Rinse under cold
water; drain.
4 Bring broth, sauce and sake to the boil in
large saucepan.
5 Divide noodles and broth among bowls; top
with mushrooms and remaining ingredients.
Serve with seven-spice mix and chilli sesame
oil, if you like.
soy broth Place bones in large saucepan;
cover with water. Bring to the boil; drain.
Rinse bones; return to saucepan. Add
remaining ingredients; cover with water by
5cm (2 inches). Bring to the boil; remove and
discard seaweed. Simmer about 5 hours or
until liquid has reduced to 1.5 litres (6 cups);
strain into large bowl. Refrigerate broth until
cold; discard fat from surface.
tips To help the kelp release its flavour, make a few
cuts along the edge with a pair of scissors.
It's best to make the broth the day before; it needs
to chill long enough for the fat to solidify on top.

RAMEN, PORK AND SPINACH SOUP

prep + cook time **1 hour 35 minutes**
(+ refrigeration) serves **4**
nutritional count per serving **12.4g total fat**
(4.8g saturated fat); 1680kJ (402 cal);
40.1g carbohydrate; 26.6g protein; 4.5g fibre

1kg (2 pounds) chicken necks
3 litres (12 cups) water
1 large leek (500g), chopped coarsely
5cm (2-inch) piece fresh ginger (25g),
    sliced thinly
10 black peppercorns
¼ cup (60ml) japanese soy sauce
¼ cup (60ml) sake
1 teaspoon sesame oil
250g (8 ounces) fresh ramen noodles
300g (9½ ounces) spinach, trimmed,
    chopped coarsely
200g (6½ ounces) chinese barbecued pork,
    sliced thinly
1 fresh long red chilli, sliced thinly
½ sheet toasted seaweed (yaki-nori),
    cut into small pieces

1 Bring chicken, the water, leek, ginger and peppercorns to the boil in large saucepan. Reduce heat; simmer, uncovered, 1 hour. Strain broth through muslin-lined sieve into large heatproof bowl; discard solids. Allow broth to cool. Cover; refrigerate until cold.
2 Discard fat from surface of broth; return broth to same cleaned pan, bring to the boil. Stir in sauce, sake and oil; return to the boil. Remove from heat.
3 Meanwhile, cook noodles in large saucepan of boiling water until tender; drain. Rinse under cold water; drain.
4 Divide noodles, spinach, pork, chilli and seaweed among bowls; ladle over broth.
tip It's best to make the broth the day before; it needs to chill long enough for the fat to solidify on top.

VEGETARIAN SUKIYAKI

prep + cook time 30 minutes serves 4
nutritional count per serving 11.9g total fat
(2.5g saturated fat); 2232kJ (534 cal);
65.8g carbohydrate; 29g protein; 9.4g fibre

350g (11 ounces) firm tofu
440g (14 ounces) fresh udon noodles
8 fresh shiitake mushrooms
4 green onions (scallions), cut into chunks
100g (3 ounces) baby spinach leaves
230g (7 ounces) canned bamboo
    shoots, drained
350g (11 ounces) wombok (napa cabbage),
    chopped coarsely
100g (3 ounces) enoki mushrooms, trimmed
1 small leek (200g), chopped coarsely
2 medium carrots (240g), sliced thickly
4 eggs
broth
1 cup (250ml) japanese soy sauce
½ cup (125ml) sake
½ cup (125ml) mirin
1 cup (250ml) water
½ cup (110g) caster (superfine) sugar

1 Press tofu between two chopping boards
with weight on top, raise one end; stand
25 minutes. Cut into 2cm (¾-inch) cubes.
2 Rinse noodles under hot water; drain.
Cut into random lengths.
3 Make broth.
4 Meanwhile, remove and discard mushroom
stems; cut a cross in top of caps.
5 Arrange all ingredients, except eggs, on
serving platters or in bowls. Place broth in
medium bowl.
6 Break eggs into individual bowls; beat lightly.
7 Pour broth into sukiyaki pan (or electric frying
pan). Heat pan on portable gas cooker at the
table; cook a quarter of the noodles and a
quarter of the remaining ingredients in broth,
uncovered, until just tender. Dip cooked
ingredients into egg before eating. Repeat
process until all the remaining noodles and
ingredients are cooked.
broth Stir ingredients in medium saucepan
over heat until sugar dissolves.

tip Sukiyaki pans are available from Japanese stores.

VEGETABLES

VEGETABLE TEMPURA

prep + cook time **40 minutes** serves **4**
nutritional count per serving **39.6g total fat**
(5.7g saturated fat); 3285kJ (786 cal);
78.3g carbohydrate; 20.3g protein; 11.7g fibre

250g (8 ounces) firm tofu
1 medium brown onion (150g)
1 small fresh or frozen lotus root (200g)
8 fresh shiitake mushrooms
2 sheets toasted seaweed (yaki-nori)
20g (¾ ounce) cellophane noodles,
    cut in half
vegetable oil, for deep-frying
plain (all-purpose) flour, for dusting
120g (4 ounces) pumpkin, sliced
50g (1½ ounces) green beans, halved
1 small kumara (orange sweet potato) (250g),
    sliced thinly
1 baby eggplant (60g), sliced
1 small red capsicum (bell pepper) (150g),
    seeded, cut into squares
1 medium carrot (120g), sliced
1 medium lemon (140g), cut into wedges
batter
1 egg, beaten lightly
2 cups (500ml) iced soda water
1 cup (150g) plain (all-purpose) flour
1 cup (150g) cornflour (cornstarch)

1 Press tofu between two chopping boards with weight on top, raise one end; stand 25 minutes. Cut into 2cm (¾-inch) cubes.
2 Halve onion through root end. Insert toothpicks at regular intervals to hold onion rings together; slice in between.
3 Peel lotus root and slice; place in water with a dash of vinegar to prevent browning. (If using canned lotus, drain and slice.) Discard mushroom stems; cut a cross in top of caps.
4 Cut one sheet nori into 5cm (2-inch) squares; halve other sheet, cut into 2cm (¾-inch) wide strips. Brush nori strips with water, wrap tightly around middle of 10 noodles; reserve noodle bundles.
5 Make batter.
6 Heat oil in large saucepan; deep-fry noodle bundles. Meanwhile, dust tofu and vegetables lightly in flour; shake off excess. Dip tofu, vegetables and nori squares in batter; drain excess. Deep-fry, in batches, until golden; drain. (Only fry in small batches; ensure oil comes back to correct temperature before adding next batch.)
7 Serve tempura and noodles immediately with lemon and tempura dipping sauce (see recipe, page 7), with a little grated daikon, if you like.
batter Combine egg and soda water in bowl. Add sifted flours at once; mix lightly until just combined. Do not overmix; mixture should be lumpy.

SESAME TOFU SALAD

prep + cook time 35 minutes (+ standing) serves 4
nutritional count per serving 59.7g total fat
(9.9g saturated fat); 2796kJ (699 cal);
9.2g carbohydrate; 22.8g protein; 6.2g fibre

2 x 300g (9½-ounce) blocks silken firm tofu
2 tablespoons sesame seeds, toasted
2 tablespoons kalonji
2 teaspoons dried chilli flakes
2 tablespoons cornflour (cornstarch)
vegetable oil, for deep-frying
100g (3 ounces) red oak lettuce leaves, torn
100g (3 ounces) mizuna
5 green onions (scallions), sliced thinly
1 large avocado (320g), chopped coarsely
1 fresh long red chilli, sliced thinly
sesame dressing
2 shallots (50g), chopped finely
2 tablespoons white sesame seeds, toasted
1 tablespoon sesame oil
1 tablespoon kecap manis
1cm (½-inch) piece fresh ginger (5g), grated
¼ cup (60ml) lemon juice

1 Press tofu between two chopping boards
with weight on top, raise one end; stand
25 minutes.
2 Meanwhile, make sesame dressing.
3 Cut each tofu block lengthways into four
slices; pat dry with absorbent paper. Combine
seeds, chilli and cornflour in large shallow
bowl; press seed mixture onto both sides of
tofu slices.
4 Heat oil in medium saucepan; deep-fry
tofu, in batches, until golden. Drain on
absorbent paper.
5 Place remaining ingredients in large bowl;
toss gently to combine. Divide salad
among serving plates; top with tofu, drizzle
with dressing.
sesame dressing Place ingredients in
screw-top jar; shake well.

omelette salad

OMELETTE SALAD

prep + cook time 25 minutes serves 4
nutritional count per serving 6.8g total fat
(1.9g saturated fat); 744kJ (178 cal);
13.4g carbohydrate; 11.9g protein; 6.8g fibre

4 eggs
1 tablespoon japanese soy sauce
½ sheet toasted seaweed (yaki-nori),
    sliced thinly
1 medium daikon (600g)
2 medium carrots (240g)
6 large red radishes (210g), sliced thinly
120g (4 ounces) red cabbage, shredded finely
1½ cups (120g) bean sprouts, trimmed
2 tablespoons (46g) drained pink pickled
    ginger, sliced thinly
6 green onions (scallions), sliced thinly
wasabi dressing
2 tablespoons japanese soy sauce
1 tablespoon pink pickled ginger juice
1 tablespoon mirin
1 teaspoon wasabi paste

1 Make wasabi dressing.
2 Combine egg, sauce and seaweed in small jug. Pour half of the egg mixture into large heated oiled frying pan; cook, uncovered, until just set. Slide omelette onto plate; roll into cigar shape. Slice omelette roll into thin rings. Repeat with remaining egg mixture.
3 Using vegetable peeler, slice daikon and carrot into thin strips. Place in large bowl with remaining ingredients; toss to combine. Divide salad among serving dishes; top with omelette rings and, if you like, extra green onion.
wasabi dressing Place ingredients in screw-top jar; shake well.

FIVE-COLOURED SALAD

prep + cook time 30 minutes (+ standing) serves 4
nutritional count per serving 9.9g total fat
(1.3g saturated fat); 765kJ (183 cal);
9.6g carbohydrate; 9.7g protein; 7.7g fibre

6 dried shiitake mushrooms
115g (3½ ounces) green beans
120g (4 ounces) daikon, cut into matchsticks
1 medium carrot (120g), cut into matchsticks
8 dried apricots, sliced thinly
1 teaspoon finely shredded lemon rind
tofu dressing
200g (6½ ounces) firm tofu
2 tablespoons tahini
1 tablespoon rice vinegar
1 tablespoon mirin
2 teaspoons caster (superfine) sugar
2 teaspoons japanese soy sauce

1 Place mushrooms in small heatproof bowl, cover with boiling water, stand 20 minutes; drain. Discard stems; slice caps thinly.
2 Meanwhile, make tofu dressing.
3 Meanwhile, quarter beans lengthways; cut into chunks. Boil, steam or microwave beans, daikon and carrot, separately, until just tender; drain. Rinse under cold water; drain.
4 Combine mushrooms, beans, daikon, carrot, apricots and dressing. Sprinkle with rind.
tofu dressing Press tofu between two chopping boards with weight on top, raise one end; stand 25 minutes. Blend or process tofu until smooth, place in bowl; stir in tahini. Add remaining ingredients; stir until sugar dissolves.

five-coloured salad

SOYA BEANS AND VEGETABLES

prep + cook time **5 hours 30 minutes**
(+ standing) serves **8**
nutritional count per serving **23.9g total fat**
(5.7g saturated fat); 1969kJ (471 cal);
24.9g carbohydrate; 23.7g protein; 16.5g fibre

2¼ cups (450g) dried soya beans
10cm (4-inch) piece kelp (konbu)
2 cloves garlic, bruised
3 bay leaves
¼ cup (60ml) olive oil
40g (1½ ounces) butter
2 large onions (400g), chopped
3 medium carrots (360g), chopped
2 stalks celery (300g), chopped
½ small daikon (250g), chopped
3 baby eggplants (180g), chopped
1½ tablespoons plain (all-purpose) flour
¾ cup (185ml) mirin
½ cup (125ml) sake
3 cups (750ml) vegetable stock
400g (12½-ounces) canned diced tomatoes
2 tablespoons red miso
2 tablespoons japanese soy sauce
1 tablespoon chopped fresh thyme
2cm (¾-inch) piece fresh ginger (10g), grated
1 teaspoon finely grated lemon rind
1½ cups (90g) japanese breadcrumbs
2 tablespoons finely chopped fresh
    flat-leaf parsley

1 Soak beans and kelp in cold water overnight; drain. Discard kelp.
2 Place beans, garlic and two of the bay leaves in large saucepan with enough water to cover; bring to the boil. Reduce heat; simmer 2½ hours or until tender. Drain. Rinse under cold water; drain.
3 Preheat oven to 180°C/350°F.
4 Heat half the oil and half the butter with remaining bay leaf in large saucepan; cook onion, stirring, 15 minutes. Remove from pan.
5 Add a little more oil to pan; cook carrot, celery and daikon, stirring occasionally, 15 minutes or until golden. Remove from pan.
6 Add remaining oil; cook eggplant, stirring, 5 minutes. Remove from pan.
7 Melt remaining butter in pan; cook flour, stirring, 1 minute. Whisk in mirin and sake until smooth. Stir in stock, undrained tomatoes, miso, sauce, thyme, ginger and rind. Bring to the boil, then simmer until thickened slightly.
8 Place beans, vegetables and sauce in 5-litre (20-cup) ovenproof dish; bake, covered, 2 hours. Sprinkle with breadcrumbs and parsley; bake, uncovered, further 30 minutes or until golden. Serve with japanese mayonnaise, if you like.

AO-NORI also known as green laver. A type of edible green seaweed, it is used in its dried form for Japanese soups and tempura.

BEAN SPROUTS also called bean shoots; tender new growths of beans and seeds, germinated for consumption as sprouts.

BEANS

green also known as french or string beans (although the tough string they once had has generally been bred out of them). This long, thin, fresh bean is consumed in its entirety once cooked.

snake long (about 40cm), thin, round, fresh, green beans, Asian in origin, with a taste similar to green or french beans. Used most frequently in stir-fries, they are also known as yard-long beans because of their (pre-metric) length.

BEEF, EYE FILLET STEAKS also known as beef tenderloin or fillet.

BREADCRUMBS, JAPANESE also called panko; lighter texture than Western-style ones. There are two kinds: larger pieces and fine crumbs. Available from Asian food stores and some supermarkets.

BUK CHOY, BABY also known as pak kat farang or shanghai bok *choy*; much smaller and more tender than regular buk choy. Its mildly acrid, distinctively appealing taste has made it one of the most commonly used asian greens.

BUTTER we use salted or unsalted (sweet) butter; 125g is equal to one stick of butter.

CAPSICUM also known as bell pepper; seeds and membranes should be discarded before use. Available in several colours, each of which has an individual flavour.

CHICKEN

breast fillet skinned, boned chicken breast.

neck bony cut, used to make chicken stock or broth.

thigh fillets skinned and boned chicken thigh.

CHILLI

bean paste made from fermented soy beans and hot chillis; red-brown in colour.

dried flakes also sold as crushed chilli; dehydrated, deep red, extremely fine slices and whole seeds. Good for cooking or for sprinkling over cooked food.

long red available both fresh and dried. A generic term for any moderately hot, long, thin chilli (about 6cm to 8cm long).

paste blend of hot chillis, oil, garlic and salt.

red thai small, hot, bright-red chilli.

CORIANDER also called cilantro, pak chee or chinese parsley; herb with bright green leaves, having both pungent aroma and taste. Used as an ingredient in a wide variety of cuisines. Often stirred into or sprinkled over a dish just before serving for maximum impact as, like other leafy herbs, its characteristics diminish with cooking. Both the stems and roots of coriander are used in some dishes; wash well before chopping. Coriander seeds are dried and sold either whole or ground, and neither form tastes remotely like the fresh leaf.

CORNFLOUR also known as cornstarch. Available made from corn or wheat (wheaten cornflour, gluten-free, gives a lighter texture in cakes); used as a thickening agent in cooking.

DAIKON also called white radish; an everyday fixture at the Japanese table. This long, white horseradish has a fresh and mild flavour when eaten raw and a wonderful, sweet flavour when cooked. After peeling, add it to salads or shred to use as a garnish; also great when sliced or cubed and cooked in stir-fries and casseroles. The flesh is white but the skin can be either white or black; buy those that are firm and unwrinkled from Asian food shops. Store wrapped in plastic in the refrigerator.

DASHI the basic fish-and-seaweed stock that accounts for the distinctive flavour of many Japanese dishes, such as soups and various casserole dishes. Made from dried bonito (a type of tuna) flakes and kombu (kelp); instant dashi (dashi-no-moto) is available in powder, granules and liquid concentrate from Asian food shops.

EGGPLANT also called aubergine; spongy flesh and mild flavour. Can be roasted, grilled or sauteed.

EGGS some recipes in this book may call for raw or barely cooked eggs; exercise caution if there is a salmonella problem in your area.

FIVE-SPICE POWDER usually a fragrant mixture of ground cinnamon, cloves, star anise, sichuan pepper and fennel seeds but the ingredients vary from country to country. Five-spice is used extensively in Chinese and other Asian cooking; available from most supermarkets or Asian food shops.

FLOUR, PLAIN also known as all-purpose.

GLOSSARY

GINGER

fresh also called green or root ginger; the thick gnarled root of a tropical plant. Can be kept, peeled, covered with dry sherry in a jar and refrigerated, or frozen in an airtight container.

pickled can be either pink (gari) or red (beni-shoga). The pink variety comprises paper-thin shavings of ginger pickled in a mixture of vinegar, sugar and natural colouring; often used with sushi or rich food as a palate cleanser. Pickled red strips are used in sushi rolls. Available from Asian food shops.

KALONJI also called nigella or black onion seeds; often erroneously called black cumin seeds. Tiny, angular seeds, black on the outside and creamy within, with sharp, nutty flavour that is enhanced by frying briefly in a dry, hot pan. Typically sprinkled over turkish bread immediately after baking or as an important spice in Indian cooking, kalonji can be found in Asian and most Middle Eastern food shops.

KECAP MANIS a dark, thick, sweet soy sauce used in most South-East Asian cuisines. Depending on the manufacturer, its sweetness is derived from the addition of palm sugar or molasses when brewed.

KONBU dried kelp, the basis of dashi. Sold in wide strips, it often has a white powdery substance that coats the surface. Wipe with damp cloth to discard any grit but do not wipe clean or rinse, to avoid removing surface flavour. Develops a bitter flavour if overcooked, so always remove just before water boils. To enhance flavour, cut along edges before adding to water.

KOSHIHIKARI also known as japanese rice. Small, round-grain white rice. If you are unable to buy koshihikari, you can substitute white short-grain rice and cook by the absorption method.

LEBANESE CUCUMBERS also known as the european or burpless cucumber; long, slender and thin-skinned.

MIRIN a japanese champagne-coloured cooking wine; made of glutinous rice and alcohol. It is used expressly for cooking and should not be confused with sake. A seasoned sweet mirin, *manjo mirin*, made of water, rice, corn syrup and alcohol, is used in various Japanese dipping sauces.

MISO fermented soybean paste. There are many types of miso, each with its own aroma, flavour, colour and texture; it can be kept, airtight, for up to a year in the refrigerator. Generally, the darker the miso, the saltier the taste and denser the texture. Salt-reduced miso is available. Buy in tubs or plastic packs.

MIZUNA japanese green vegetable with tender leaves and peppery flavour. If you are unable to find mizuna, you can substitute mustard greens or rocket.

MUSHROOMS

button small, cultivated white mushrooms with a mild flavour. When we call for an unspecified type of mushroom, use button.

enoki long, thin and white in colour; available fresh or tinned.

shiitake, dried also called donko or dried chinese mushrooms; have a unique, meaty flavour. Sold dried; rehydrate before use.

shiitake, fresh also known as chinese black, forest or golden oak mushrooms. Although cultivated, they have the earthiness and taste of wild mushrooms.

MUSTARD

japanese hot mustard in ready-to-use paste in tubes, or powder form, from Asian food shops.

wholegrain also known as seeded. A french-style coarse-grain mustard made from crushed mustard seeds and dijon-style french mustard.

NOODLES

cellophane also known as chinese vermicelli, bean threads, bean-thread noodles, crystal noodles and glass noodles. Made from a starch, such as potato, mung bean or cassava – not rice – they are generally sold dry and reconstituted by boiling or soaking in water. They are transparent, hence the name.

dried wheat made of wheat flour; usually white in colour.

ramen made of wheat and egg; firm textured and yellowish in colour.

soba thin, pale-brown noodles originally from Japan; made from buckwheat and varying proportions of wheat flour. Available dried and fresh, and in flavoured (for instance, green tea) varieties. Eaten in soups, stir-fries and, chilled, on their own.

somen very thin white wheat noodles.

udon available fresh and dried; broad, white, wheat noodles, the thickest of the Japanese varieties.

NORI a type of dried seaweed used as a Japanese flavouring, garnish or for sushi. Sold in thin sheets, plain or toasted (see *yaki-nori*).

OMELETTE consists of beaten egg cooked with butter or oil in a frying pan, often folded around a filling.

PARSLEY, FLAT LEAF also known as continental or italian parsley.

PORK

chinese barbecued also called char siew. Has a sweet, sticky coating made from soy sauce, sherry, five-spice powder and hoisin sauce. Available from Asian food stores.

fillet skinless, boneless eye fillet cut from the loin.

minced ground lean pork.

RICE, JAPANESE *see koshihikari.*

SAKE Japan's favourite wine, made from fermented rice; used for marinating, cooking and as part of dipping sauces. If sake is unavailable, dry sherry, vermouth or brandy can be substituted. If drinking sake, stand it first in a container in hot water for 20 minutes to warm it through.

SHALLOT also called french shallot, golden shallot or eschalot. Small and elongated, with a brown skin, they grow in tight clusters similar to garlic.

SASHIMI raw fish or meat.

SAUCES

hoisin a thick, sweet and spicy chinese barbecue sauce made from salted, fermented soybeans, onions and garlic; used as a marinade or baste, or to accent stir-fries and barbecued or roasted foods. Available from Asian food shops and supermarkets.

soy also known as sieu; made from fermented soybeans. Several variations are available; we use japanese soy sauce unless indicated otherwise.

teriyaki sweet soy sauce; used as a marinade.

worcestershire thin, dark brown, spicy sauce developed by the British when in India; used as a seasoning for meat, gravies and cocktails, and as a condiment.

japanese worcestershire two types available – one similar to normal worcestershire and the other somewhat blander. Both are made from varying proportions of vinegar, tomatoes, onions, carrots, garlic and spices.

SESAME SEEDS small seeds, oval in shape; most commonly, black and white, but also red and brown varieties. The seeds are used as both an ingredient and a condiment. Roast the seeds in a heavy-based frying pan over low heat.

SPINACH also known as english spinach and, incorrectly, silver beet. Baby spinach leaves are best eaten raw in salads; the larger leaves should be added last to soups, stews and stir-fries, and should be cooked until they are barely wilted.

SQUID a type of mollusc, also known as calamari. Buy squid hoods to make preparation easier.

SUGAR

brown a soft, finely granulated sugar retaining molasses for its characteristic colour and flavour.

caster also known as superfine or finely granulated table sugar.

SUSHI vinegared rice, usually topped with seafood (often raw) and vegetables, or put in rolls.

SUGAR SNAP PEAS also called honey snap peas; fresh small pea which can be eaten whole.

SUKIYAKI dish cooked in one pot, often at the table. It may comprise meat and vegetables or just vegetables.

TAHINI sesame-seed paste; available from Middle Eastern food stores.

TAT SOI, BABY small variety of a popular asian green vegetable, with spoon-shaped leaves and distinctive flavour.

TOFU also known as soybean curd or bean curd; off-white, custard-like product made from the "milk" of crushed soybeans. Comes fresh (soft or firm), and processed (fried or pressed dried sheets). Fresh tofu can be refrigerated in water (changed daily) for up to four days.

TONKATSU deep-fried crumbed pork cutlet.

WAKAME a highly nutritious seaweed; black when purchased dried but reconstitutes to bright green. Soak for only 5 minutes or it will go mushy. Leaves are usually stripped from central vein.

WASABI also called wasabe; an asian horseradish used to make the pungent, green-coloured sauce traditionally served with Japanese raw fish dishes. Sold in powdered or paste form.

WOMBOK also known as chinese cabbage, peking or napa cabbage; elongated in shape with pale green, crinkly leaves. The most common cabbage in South-East Asia. Can be shredded or chopped and eaten raw or braised, steamed or stir-fried.

YAKI-NORI pre-toasted seaweed. Yaki means grilled or fried and nori is dried laver seaweed. It is commonly used to wrap sushi.

CONVERSION CHART

MEASURES

One Australian metric measuring cup holds approximately 250ml, one Australian metric tablespoon holds 20ml, one Australian metric teaspoon holds 5ml.

The difference between one country's measuring cups and another's is within a 2- or 3-teaspoon variance, and will not affect your cooking results. North America, New Zealand and the United Kingdom use a 15ml tablespoon. All cup and spoon measurements are level. The most accurate way of measuring dry ingredients is to weigh them. When measuring liquids, use a clear glass or plastic jug with metric markings.

We use large eggs with an average weight of 60g.

DRY MEASURES

METRIC	IMPERIAL
15g	½oz
30g	1oz
60g	2oz
90g	3oz
125g	4oz (¼lb)
155g	5oz
185g	6oz
220g	7oz
250g	8oz (½lb)
280g	9oz
315g	10oz
345g	11oz
375g	12oz (¾lb)
410g	13oz
440g	14oz
470g	15oz
500g	16oz (1lb)
750g	24oz (1½lb)
1kg	32oz (2lb)

LIQUID MEASURES

METRIC	IMPERIAL
30ml	1 fluid oz
60ml	2 fluid oz
100ml	3 fluid oz
125ml	4 fluid oz
150ml	5 fluid oz
190ml	6 fluid oz
250ml	8 fluid oz
300ml	10 fluid oz
500ml	16 fluid oz
600ml	20 fluid oz
1000ml (1 litre)	1¾ pints

LENGTH MEASURES

METRIC	IMPERIAL
3mm	⅛in
6mm	¼in
1cm	½in
2cm	¾in
2.5cm	1in
5cm	2in
6cm	2½in
8cm	3in
10cm	4in
13cm	5in
15cm	6in
18cm	7in
20cm	8in
23cm	9in
25cm	10in
28cm	11in
30cm	12in (1ft)

OVEN TEMPERATURES

These oven temperatures are only a guide for conventional ovens.
For fan-forced ovens, check the manufacturer's manual.

	°C (CELSIUS)	°F (FAHRENHEIT)
Very slow	120	250
Slow	150	300
Moderately slow	160	325
Moderate	180	350
Moderately hot	200	400
Hot	220	425
Very hot	240	475

The imperial measurements used in these recipes are approximate only and should not affect your cooking results.

B
batter (vegetable tempura) 66
beef
  salad 8
  sesame-roasted steak 44
  teppanyaki 46
  teriyaki platter 48
bonito flakes 4
breadcrumbs, japanese (panko) 4
broth 64
  somen and dashi 18
  soy 61

C
california rolls 22
chicken
  and noodle salad 30
  grilled miso 29
  steamed chicken salad with
    sesame sauce 33
  teppanyaki (mixed barbecue) 46
  yakitori 14
chilli dressing 44

D
dipping sauce 46
  ginger and lemon 43
  tempura 7
dressing
  chilli 44
  mustard and soy 8
  ponzu 29
  sesame 69
  sesame and peanut 30
  tofu 70
  wasabi 70
duck
  crisp duck breast with orange
    and daikon salad 29
  sake duck with snow peas
    and avocado 26

E
eggs
  egg drop soup 17
  omelette salad 70
  thick omelette 18

F
five-coloured salad 70
fried noodles 58
fried soba 54

G
ginger and lemon dipping sauce
  43
ginger, pickled 7
gomasio (sesame salt) 6
gyozas (pot stickers)14

H
hand-moulded sushi 10
hot pot, seafood 40

J
japanese ingredients 4
japanese essentials 6

K
konbu (dried kelp) 5

M
miso 5
  grilled miso chicken 29
  red miso sauce 6
mixed barbecue (teppenyaki) 46
mustard and soy dressing 8

N
noodles
  chicken and noodle salad 30
  fried 58
  fried soba 54
  ramen noodles with soy broth 61
  ramen, pork and spinach soup 62
  seafood and udon
    noodle stir-fry 34
  soba noodles with pork,
    eggplant and chilli 58
  somen and dashi broth 18
  udon noodle soup 56

O
omelette
  salad 70
  thick 18

P
panko (japanese breadcrumbs) 4
pepper, japanese 4
pickled ginger 7
ponzu dressing 29
pork
  deep-fried crumbed
    pork (tonkatsu) 52
  fried noodles 58
  fried soba 54
  gyozas (pot stickers) 12
  japanese pork stir-fry 51
  ramen, pork and
    spinach soup 62
  soba noodles with pork,
    eggplant and chilli 58
  stir-fried pork and ginger
    cabbage 48
  teriyaki pork with
    pineapple 51
pot stickers (gyozas) 14

Q
quail, sake-marinated 30

R
ramen noodles with soy broth 61
ramen, pork and spinach soup 62
red miso sauce 6
rice, sushi 13

S
sake duck with snow peas
  and avocado 26
sake-glazed salmon 39
sake-marinated quail 30